ESTHER

- Was chosen by the king of Persia to become the new queen
- Bravely asked the king to rescue her people
- Cared more about saving the lives of her people than her own safety

MARY

- Was willing to serve God in any way He said
- Loved and took care of her son Jesus
- Fulfilled an Old Testament prophecy (Isaiah 7:14)

PETER

- Was one of Jesus' disciples and closest friends
- Served as the first leader of the early church
- Was the first to teach Jesus' good news after Jesus rose from the dead

PAUL

- Went from arresting Christians to becoming a Christian
- Led many people to come to know Jesus
- Wrote at least thirteen books of the Bible

TIMOTHY

- Joined Paul on trips to teach Jesus' good news to more people
- Was taught by Paul and became like a son to him
- Led a new church at a young age

JESUS

- Fulfilled Old Testament prophecies (matched up exactly with what God had said the Savior would be)
- Is the Son of God from heaven, sent to the world to show what God is like and to rescue people from their sin
- Died on the cross and rose from the dead to make a way for people to be forgiven and have life with God forever

TO:

_____

FROM:

_____

DATE:

_____

Little Faithfuls

You're So Brave

Written by Carrie Marrs

Illustrated by Christiane Engel

An Imprint of Thomas Nelson

God's big story of bravery started a long time ago when God made the whole world with His amazing power. He made tall mountains and deep oceans, roaring lions and fast horses, mighty eagles and huge whales. God imagined and created all of them.

When God made people, He wanted them to be strong and brave like Him. He wanted them to do hard things—even when they felt scared. He wanted them to believe He would take care of them no matter what.

So He started giving them chances to be brave with His help. They would have the chance to do something good but a little scary. They would have to trust God in order to do that good, hard thing—and their bravery would grow.

Before too long, many people started becoming brave with God.

Abraham was one of those people.

God said to Abraham, "Go to a new land I'll show you. I want to give you a new home and bless you, and I'll take care of you along the way."

Abraham didn't know where he would end up, but he believed God's promises to take care of him. So Abraham, along with his wife and nephew, packed up their things and bravely headed to a new country.

Abraham's great-great-great-great grandson was named Moses. God gave Moses a job that seemed pretty scary. He said, "Go tell Pharaoh to free My people."

"Me?" Moses said. "I don't think I can do that!"

"Don't worry," God said. "I'll be with you."

Moses still felt nervous but decided to try—because God was with him. He trusted in God's strength and kept standing up to Pharaoh until God's people were freed.

God's freed people needed a new home, but they had to battle the city of Jericho to get it. So two spies snuck into the city to find a way to win the fight.

When they needed a place to hide from soldiers, a woman named Rahab said, "Follow me!" and led them to a hiding spot on her roof.

Soldiers came searching, but Rahab pointed them in another direction.

Later she helped the spies escape through a window. "Grab this rope to climb down," she said.

"You've been so brave to help us!" said the spies. "When our people come back to Jericho, we'll make sure you and your family stay safe."

God's people, who were called the Israelites, went into a new land called Canaan. There came a time when they needed God to rescue them from a mean king.

God said, "If the small Israelite army will battle the big Canaanite army, I'll make sure Israel wins."

But Barak, Israel's army leader, was still afraid they'd lose. He'd only go into battle if Deborah, a brave prophet and judge who trusted God, went with him.

Deborah said, "We have God's power with us. Let's go!"

God was with them—and they won!

Years later, God's people were about to have another battle. But Israel's whole army was too afraid to fight their scary enemy—a giant named Goliath.

A young man named David surprised everyone when he said, "I'll go fight him. God will help me!" All the grown-up men were amazed as they watched young David walk up to Goliath.

"I may be weak, but my God is mighty!" cried David. Then he threw a stone at the giant's forehead and knocked him down!

A long time after that, God's people were forced to spread out and live in different places. One Israelite named Daniel was sent to Babylon.

Most people around Daniel didn't worship God, but Daniel prayed to Him every day.

Even when the king of Babylon made a new rule that said anyone who prayed to God would be thrown in the lions' den, Daniel still didn't quit praying.

Daniel ended up in the lions' den, but God protected him. "God sent His angel to close the lions' mouths," he said. "Now people can see that God is real!"

Later on, God's people had to live in a country called Persia. Esther, the queen of Persia, found out that someone was going to kill all the Israelites. She was an Israelite too, but she'd been keeping that a secret.

If she went to the king for help, she knew he might help her, or he might have her killed.

Esther bravely decided to go to the king. "Someone is trying to kill my people, the Israelites," she said. "Will you save us?"

The king said yes! Esther's bravery saved God's people.

Many years later, there was a girl named Mary who loved God very much.

One day, an angel came to Mary and said, "God is giving you a very special job—something only you will do. You will have a baby who will be the Son of God. His name will be Jesus."

Mary didn't say, "That's crazy!" or "I can't
do that!" or "How hard will this be?"
    No, Mary was brave enough to trust God.
She wanted to obey Him. Right away she said,
"I'm ready to serve God."

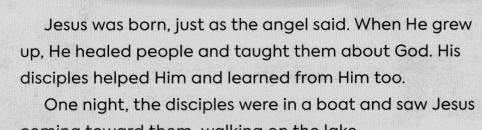

Jesus was born, just as the angel said. When He grew up, He healed people and taught them about God. His disciples helped Him and learned from Him too.

One night, the disciples were in a boat and saw Jesus coming toward them, walking on the lake.

"Peter, come to Me," Jesus said.

Peter bravely stepped out of the boat and walked on the water toward Jesus. But when Peter saw the big waves around him, he got scared and started to sink.

Jesus caught him. He said, "Keep looking at Me and trusting Me."

Later on, after Jesus went to heaven, many people who believed in Him became brave as they lived like Him.

When Paul was put in jail for serving God, he didn't get mad at God.

Instead, right in his jail cell, he sang praise songs to God. Paul was so happy to be God's friend, and he knew God was taking care of him, even in jail.

Paul's example of bravery helped the jailer become a follower of Jesus.

Timothy was another person who became brave as he followed Jesus.

Paul gave Timothy the big job of leading a new church. But Timothy felt afraid, especially when people said he was too young to be a leader.

"You're young, but you can still do important things for God," Paul said. "He gives you a spirit of power, not fear."

Timothy believed that God would help him, and he led the church for several years.

Ever since those first believers, Jesus'
followers have remembered His bravery.

When Jesus was about to go to the cross to
die for our sins, He felt so afraid.

He could've done whatever His feelings told
Him to do. But instead, Jesus trusted that God's
plan was best, even though it was scary.

"I feel like doing something easier," He prayed, "but I know You're always right. So I will do whatever You want."

Jesus bravely said yes to the scariest thing, and He saved the world.

God makes His people brave and uses His brave people for doing good in the world. He has important things meant especially for you to do!

So don't let fear stop you from growing stronger. Face hard things with bravery so you can do important things for God.

Try something new or keep working at something hard, like learning to ride a bike. Raise your hand to be

a volunteer or go play with someone who is alone. Tell the truth. Forgive a friend. Each time you do something brave, you'll get braver.

Remember, God is mighty, and He can show you how to be brave. He'll help you! No matter where you are or where you go, He will be with you.

Little Faithfuls: You're So Brave

© 2020 Thomas Nelson

Tommy Nelson, PO Box 141000, Nashville, TN 37214

All rights reserved. No portion of this book may be reproduced, stored in a retrieval system, or transmitted in any form or by any means—electronic, mechanical, photocopy, recording, scanning, or other—except for brief quotations in critical reviews or articles, without the prior written permission of the publisher.

Published in Nashville, Tennessee, by Tommy Nelson. Tommy Nelson is an imprint of Thomas Nelson. Thomas Nelson is a registered trademark of HarperCollins Christian Publishing, Inc.

Tommy Nelson titles may be purchased in bulk for educational, business, fund-raising, or sales promotional use. For information, please e-mail SpecialMarkets@ThomasNelson.com.

ISBN 978-1-4002-1925-4 (eBook)

 Library of Congress Cataloging-in-Publication Data is on file.
ISBN 978-1-4002-1898-1

Written by Carrie Marrs

Illustrated by Christiane Engel

Printed in China
20 21 22 23 24   DSC   10 9 8 7 6 5 4 3 2 1

Mfr: DSC / Shenzhen, China / July 2020 / PO #9585487

ABRAHAM

- Started a new nation in Canaan
- Believed God would give him a baby even when he and his wife were too old
- Had a family that grew into the people of God (who showed the world what God was like)

MOSES

- Led God's people out of Egypt
- Split the Red Sea so God's people could escape Pharaoh's army
- Gave God's Ten Commandments to Israel

RAHAB

- Risked her life to help keep the Israelite spies safe
- Tied a red rope to her window to mark it as a place to keep safe when the Israelites returned
- Was an ancestor of Jesus

DEBORAH

- Led Israel's army to victory
- Was the only woman in Israel to serve as a judge (someone wise who helped people know what to do when they had problems)
- Was a prophet (someone close to God who shared His messages with others)

DAVID

- Defeated the giant Goliath when he was young
- Wrote many psalms (praise songs to God)
- Served as king of Israel

DANIEL

- Served as a special helper to kings (helping them make important decisions)
- Kept worshipping God when almost no one else around him was
- Stayed loyal to God even when his life was in danger